Some Basics About

KARATE

By Ed and Ruth Radlauer

Gemini Series

AN ELK GROVE BOOK

CHILDRENS PRESS ™

CHICAGO

**Created for CHILDRENS PRESS
by Radlauer Productions, Incorporated**

Credits:
For technical assistance, photographic assistance,
and authentication, the author thanks Ray Dalke of
West Coast Karate Association, Riverside, California
and University of California at Riverside.

Library of Congress Cataloging in Publication Data

Radlauer, Ed.
  Some basics about karate.

  (Gemini series)
  "An Elk Grove book."
  Summary: Introduces a martial art that helps the
mind and body work together and helps one defend one-
self against an attacker.
  1. Karate—Juvenile literature. [1. Karate]
I. Radlauer, Ruth Shaw. II. Title.
GV1114.3.R32   796.8'153   81-2743
ISBN 0-516-07694-9   AACR2

#7378167

Contents

Karate

It's a sport that builds your body. It helps your mind control your body. And it's a martial art that helps you defend yourself against attack. Yes, the martial art of karate does all this and more.

If you learn karate, you will build your body and help your mind and body to work together better. You'll be able to defend yourself against an attacker.

You will also improve other skills. Body control can make you a sharper ball player, a faster runner, a stronger athlete. Besides improving skills and learning to defend yourself, karate helps you think faster and work longer.

Karate can also help you understand what is fair and unfair, right or wrong. You will understand more about people and the world around you.

Is karate a new sport? No, it started long ago and not as a sport.

A Long Time Ago

It was a very long time ago in the land of China. A man was trying to teach others to sit quietly, think, and lead simple lives. But things were not going too well.

After a while the teacher, Bhodidharma, noticed his students, religious monks, were getting weak. These weak monks could not defend themselves against attacking bandits. To help them, Bhodidharma taught them breathing exercises and control of the body. The monks gained strength and developed ways to defend themselves from bandit attacks.

From this beginning hundreds of years ago, karate developed into the art we know today. For a while in China it was a secret art. But the secret skills of karate spread to other lands where it was call karate-jitsu, art of the hands.

Today's karate is the result of work done by Funakoshi Gichin. He began studying karate in Okinawa at the age of eleven. As a man, Funakoshi demonstrated karate in Japan. Soon the art became popular not only in Japan, but all over the world.

Empty Hands

No gun. No knife. No rock or stick. In karate you defend yourself without the use of a gun, rock, or stick.

When you are studying karate, everything must be fair. Both you and your opponent have empty hands. Your only weapons are your fists and feet. Because you have nothing else, you must learn to see trouble coming and avoid it.

But karate as a martial art is much more than empty hands. Karate teaches you to avoid attack. If you are attacked, karate teaches you how to turn the attack to your advantage. Karate also teaches you to develop your body as a weapon against an attacker.

All this takes a lot of training and time. Yes, you could teach yourself some karate. But the best way to learn this martial art is to go to a school with a very special name.

The Dojo

Yes, it's a school. "Do" means the way. "Jo" means the place where you learn the way, the way of karate.

Here's how you learn the way of karate in a dojo. Start with a respectful bow to the place where you will learn karate. Next bow to the sensei, the teacher or master. Why bow? Because in karate, politeness, fairness, and respect are your first lessons. Here are other lessons you'll have in the dojo.

1. Getting your mind ready for karate
2. Getting your body ready for karate
3. Stance and body balance
4. Punching techniques
5. Striking techniques
6. Blocking techniques
7. Kicking techniques
8. The gi and belts
9. Kata
10. Karateka

That's a long list of lessons. Are you ready to start with a pond of water?

Mizu-no-kokoro

It's a pond. It's quiet—smooth. Nothing moves the water. It's silent. Make your mind like a smooth, quiet pond. Your mind is a mirror—mizu-no-kokoro.

That's a good beginning in karate. Your mind must become quiet—ready for the lessons in the dojo.

As the lessons start, you must not think of such things as your dog, a fight you had with a friend, or the other students in the dojo. In karate all anger leaves you. Your mind is ready for the self defense skills that will help you in case of attack.

Next you learn tsuki-no-kokoro, "mind like the moon." Just as the moon puts light everywhere, your mind will see everywhere. You will know how to defend yourself and return the attack with your counterattack.

With your body strength and mind brought to one point, you learn kime, or focus. Everything in you is focused on your action.

With mizu-no-kokoro, tsuki-no-kokoro, and kime, you're ready for—

Calisthenics

With your mind ready, it's time for you to do some calisthenics. Is that a karate word? Yes, it's an important word because by doing calisthenics, you get your body ready for karate.

Karate people do several kinds of calisthenics or exercises. Limbering up exercises get your muscles loose, warm, and working. You limber up by moving your arms, stretching your body forward, backward, sideways.

After limbering up you do muscle strengthening exercises. These are hopping, leg lifting, kicking, deep body bending, and pushups.

Skipping a rope helps your breathing. Try to get so skilled at rope jumping that you can do two jumps for each turn of the rope.

Work out on the punching bag to help you get the feel of hitting a solid body. The solid body could be an attacker.

As you limber up, strengthen your muscles, and improve your movement and breathing skills, you'll feel ready for karate stances.

Stances (Dachi)

You're ready for your first stance, the way you hold your body and move. Heisoku-dachi is a natural way to stand straight. From this position you are ready for other karate stances.

Stances and movement are what you need for self-defense and counterattack. Here are some of the first stances, or dachi, you learn.

Kiba-dachi (side stance)—Start with feet apart, toes straight ahead. To move, bring one foot in from the side and across in front of the other foot. Then step out. Place your feet apart again. The side stance helps to defend from a side attack.

Zenkutso-dachi (forward stance)—This is for both attack and defense. Put one leg to the rear. Move forward by bringing the rear leg forward close to the other. Then step forward and out, letting the other leg push you forward.

Kokutso-dachi (back stance)—Start with your feet apart, in line, and your weight over your back leg. When you step forward to attack, keep your body weight back while your foot slides forward.

Seiken-choku-zuki

That's hard for some people to say. But seiken-choku-zuki is one of the first karate punches you'll learn in the dojo.

The seiken-choku-zuki is a straight punch. Hold your left arm out straight. Have your right hand in a fist, thumb on top, next to your hip. Now as you draw back your left arm, bring up your right arm and punch straight forward. At the last moment, turn your fist over so the thumb is down. Great power comes from drawing your left arm back while your right arm punches with a twist.

The lunge punch is a straight punch delivered as you move into a forward stance. Punch with the same arm as the forward foot.

The reverse punch is most powerful. It's delivered from the forward stance. Start with your left foot in front and your left arm out, right hand back. Shoot your right fist forward as you draw your left arm back and twist your right hip forward. Thrust from your back foot to give your fist full power for the punch.

Yama-zuki

If you want to punch with both arms and fists at once, do a yama-zuki, the "U" punch. A "U" punch is good if an attacker has grabbed your hair.

For the "U" punch or yama-zuki, your arms form a letter U with your body as you attack. One fist strikes at the opponent's head, the lower fist goes to the body area.

For the "U" punch, get into the forward stance, one fist on each hip. Now thrust your weight forward and strike out with both arms, one high, one low. The arm doing the low punch will be over your front knee and the high punch will be almost over your head. Your upper fist is thumb down, the lower fist thumb up, as your arms and body form the letter U.

Why use a yama-zuki? Because a "U" punch is very hard to block. The yama-zuki is good against someone who grabs your hair. Punches delivered to the nose and stomach will quickly show anyone that attacking you is not a very good idea.

Riken-uchi and Tettsui-uchi

Are these more punches? Yes, in a way. But riken-uchi and tettsui-uchi are strikes. A karate strike is different from a punch.

A punch is delivered in a straight line. But if you slash from the side, snapping your elbow, that's a riken-uchi, a strike. Use the snapping motion of your elbow to strike the opponent with the back of your fist. A back-fist strike can be delivered sideways or downward. When you strike, the first two knuckles of your fist hit the opponent.

You may also do the tettsui-uchi, the bottom fist strike. With the tettsui-uchi, you hit with the bottom of your fist. You can deliver the tettsui-uchi downward or to the side.

Strikes are useful if you and your attacker are close together. But it's better not to let your attacker get close. To keep your attacker at a distance, you need to do uke or—

Blocking

Blocking may be more important than any other karate skill. Your teacher has told you, "In karate, never make the first move." If you are attacked, you make the second move, uke, a block.

In uke, or blocking, you use certain arm movements and body positions to keep away the opponent's attack. Move your body so the attack misses, or use your arm to knock it away. Turn the attack into your defense. When blocking, keep your stance and balance. Block only enough to get the time you need to go into your counterattack.

Don't do anything during a block that would leave you open to another attack. As you block, plan your counterattack.

During a block, focus all your strength on the point where you are blocking. By doing this, you may cause your attacker so much pain that the attack will be over. You won't even need to use—

Kicks

In the dojo you have learned to punch, strike, and block with your hands as weapons. Now it's time to turn your feet into weapons.

To use your feet as weapons, you must kick. Balance and timing are important. And you must be fast enough to keep the opponent from grabbing your foot.

Here are some kicks that will help turn your feet into weapons.

Front snap kick—Raise your leg toward the target with your knee bent. Then snap the lower part of the raised leg upward and kick out at the opponent. Front snap kicks can be made at angles if the target moves.

Back thrust kick—Use this kick when the attack is from the rear. Bring the kicking foot to the level of the other knee. Look over your shoulder and thrust the raised heel straight back. Both snap and thrust kicks can also be done to the side.

Roundhouse kick—Raise your kicking leg with the knee out to the side and the foot back. Then swing your leg around, striking with knee or foot.

Now your hands and feet are both weapons.

Gis And Belts

People in the dojo wear gis fastened with belts. There are different colored belts for different kyu. The sensei wears a black belt. What are gi and kyu, and what do the belt colors mean?

A gi is your white karate suit. Kyu is a rank, showing how advanced a student is in karate. A beginner is unranked and wears a white belt. After about three months you take the test for 8th kyu, or yellow belt. As you get better the belt color changes from yellow to green, brown, and black. The sensei, or teacher, wears a black belt.

All the students in the dojo are quiet and respectful as they listen to the sensei.

During lessons students do kata. Kata is a series of movements. There is no opponent, but you try to see and feel one in your imagination.

More advanced students spar. They attack and defend, using all their skills.

As students put power into thrusts, they yell, or kiai. The yell makes the stomach muscles get firm. Kiai adds strength to a movement and may upset an attacker.

A Karateka

That's what you are. You have learned mizu-no-kokoro and tsuki-no-kokoro. You have mastered kime, heisoku-dachi, and more. Yes, you are a karateka.

As a karateka, you will have respect for the dojo, other karateka, and the sensei. You show respect for the rights of others. You don't let anger creep into your mind. During kata practice you kiai with the others as you strike or kick an imaginary opponent.

You control mind, breathing, and muscles so your body becomes a weapon, the empty-handed weapon.

As you go from white belt through a number of colors, you come to know karate as a way of self-defense, a sport, and a way of living. You become a better person each day of your life. You know that if you work hard, you'll soon be wearing a black belt with your gi.

Index

B belts, 8, 11, 28–30
Bhodidharma, 7
blocking, 11, 24–26
bow, 11
breathing, 15, 31

C calisthenics, 14–15
China, 6, 7

D dachi, 16, 17
dojo, 10, 11, 13, 18, 26, 28, 29, 31

F feet, 9, 26, 27
fists, 9, 19, 21, 23
focus, 13, 25

G gi, 11, 28, 29, 31
Gichin, Funakoshi, 7

H heisoku-dachi, 16, 17, 30

J Japan, 7

K karate-jitsu, 7
karateka, 11, 30, 31
kata, 11, 29, 31
kiai, 29, 31
kiba-dachi, 17
kicking, 11, 27, 31
kicks, 26, 27
kime, 13, 30
kokutso-dachi, 17
kyu, 28, 29

L limbering, 15

M mizu-no-kokoro, 12, 13, 30

O Okinawa, 7

P punches, 18–23, 26; lunge, 19; reverse, 19; straight, 19; "U," 20, 21
punching, 11
punching bag, 15

R respect, 11, 31
riken-uchi, 22, 23

S seiken-choku-zuki, 18, 19
sensei, 10, 28, 29, 31
skipping rope, 15
spar, 29
stance, 11, 16, 17; back, 17; forward, 17, 19; side 17
strike, 22, 23, 26, 27, 31; back-fist, 23; bottom-fist, 23
striking, 11

T tettsui-uchi, 22, 23
tsuki-no-kokoro, 13, 30

U Uke, 23–25

Y yama-zuki, 20, 21

Z zenkutso-dachi, 17